MW01122495

COFFEE BREAK
EVANGELISM MANUAL
WITH
DIRECTOR'S HANDBOOK

Coffee Break
Small Groups

Deb Fennema is a veteran Coffee Break and Story Hour leader. She has served as a Coffee Break regional representative and has written several Coffee Break and Story Hour resources. Fennema resides in Kenosha, Wisconsin.

Unless otherwise indicated, the Scripture quotations in this publication are from the HOLY BIBLE, NEW INTERNATIONAL VERSION, © 1973, 1978, 1984, International Bible Society. Used by permission of Zondervan Bible Publishers.

We welcome your comments. Call us at 1-800-333-8300 or e-mail us at editors@crcpublications.org.

ISBN 1-56212-553-2

10 9 8 7 6 5 4 3 2 1

contents

introduction

WHAT IS COFFEE BREAK?

Coffee Break is a small group inductive Bible study program with the purpose of leading people into a personal relationship with Jesus.

The Coffee Break ministry and accompanying Story Hour program began in 1970 on the south side of Chicago as a way to reach women and their children with the gospel of Jesus Christ. The ministry has grown to more than a thousand local programs in Canada and the United States, as well as affiliated groups in six other countries. Several churches now have groups of men and women studying together, as well as groups for men only. Although the Bible study material was designed specifically for Coffee Break, it is also used in other types of small groups, in church school, and in other adult education programs.

There are three guidelines for using the Coffee Break name:
- The program should be small-group based.
- The Bible study should be inductive.
- The purpose should be to reach the lost.

There may be times when your small groups become a bit large, or your leaders choose to do another type of Bible study, or the Lord doesn't lead any unsaved people into your group, but these should be the exceptions rather than the rule. In general, churches that wish to be affiliated with Coffee Break should follow these three guidelines.

Most Coffee Break groups are developed as part of a church's outreach program, but some are started in homes. The Coffee Break program fits well with the overall outreach strategy of a congregation, whether it is a newly planted church or an established church. Since the focus of Coffee Break is evangelism, the goal is not primarily to recruit new church members but to tell the good news of Jesus Christ. It is a welcome bonus if group members decide to join your church.

More and more churches are recognizing the benefits of developing small groups within the congregation, and the popularity of small groups has risen concurrently with the growth of Coffee Break. The goal of all small groups should be life-change, that is, the transformation of lives because of participation in a small group. The goal of Coffee Break small groups is for members to accept Christ as Savior—the ultimate life-change.

The Coffee Break small group environment provides a warm, relaxed atmosphere that encourages everyone to participate in the Bible study. Trained leaders keep the discussion low-key and nonthreatening, allowing the Holy Spirit to work in the hearts of everyone there. Refreshments add a touch of hospitality and encourage fellowship among group members. These dynamics make Coffee Break a comfortable setting for people to invite friends, family members, and neighbors who are not Christians.

One Coffee Break leader in New York was drawn by the warmth and love of a Coffee Break group almost ten years ago:

> "I came to know the Lord as my personal Savior through Coffee Break Bible study. When I was invited to attend for the first time, I responded with an immediate 'yes.' And when I stepped into the basement of Community Christian Reformed Church, I knew there was something very different there that I wanted to be a part of. About fifty women of all ages were studying God's Word and supporting each other in prayer. There was unity and acceptance that I so desired. No one seemed to care where I came from or how I got there. They were just happy that I was there."

What Is a Small Group?

A small group is an intentional face-to-face gathering varying in size, regularly meeting together, to accomplish agreed-upon purposes. Members of Coffee Break groups agree to meet weekly in a small group (generally three to twelve people) to study the Bible together. Providing a small group is one way to reach out to people who are looking for a place of belonging or support. A small group setting provides the ideal atmosphere in which to connect disconnected people.

Following Jesus means to "make disciples." That's what we do in Coffee Break. Reaching the lost is our primary purpose. Beginning in our individual "Jerusalems" and following wherever God leads us, we invite our neighbors to join us in discovering God through his Word because we are the grateful recipients of God's grace.

Within that overarching purpose of outreach, Coffee Break groups also include the four primary functions of small groups: **being together, caring together, doing together,** and **learning together.** As we build relationships with one another (being together), we discover what the Bible is all about (learning together), model Christ's love to one another (caring together), and put that love into action (doing together) as needs arise.

As Coffee Break groups grow in these four primary areas, we also see biblical small group principles permeate the entire group. Ask anyone who has been part of a vital Coffee Break group. She'll tell you she was loved and accepted *(the principle of support and belonging),* and that she felt the excitement of discovering together things that nobody in her group could discover alone *(the principle of synergism).* She will also remember what she learned when she shared in the group *(principle of learning retention).* Over time God's Word and Spirit transforms people's lives *(the principle of transformation)* and they desire to be honest and accountable to one another *(the principle of accountability),* tackling tough issues in their lives with input from caring group members *(the principle of problem solving).* Within the safe support of their group they dare to try new things *(the principle of risk-taking and experimentation)*—all with the encouragement of loving leaders who point the way to God through his Word, extend grace to those they meet, and trust God with the results.

Small Groups Meet People's Needs

- Many people are genuinely interested in learning more about spiritual things and finding answers to life's questions in the Bible. Whether those who come to Coffee Break are opening the Bible for the first time, feeling disconnected from God, or cautiously considering God's claims, they are seeking deeper spiritual meaning in their lives.
- Many people are hungry for the close relationships that can be found in Coffee Break. Their lives may be empty, lonely, and restless. We want everyone who comes to a Coffee Break group to find acceptance and belonging—a safe place to ask questions about life, about relationships, and about God and his Word.
- Many people who would not attend a church worship service will attend a Coffee Break group. Small groups can provide an entry point for people who are wary of the established church. When people develop relationships with others in a small group, they are more open and ready to develop a relationship with God, and they become more willing to attend worship with the people they have learned to love and trust. In Coffee Break people find a place to grow in their faith as they are encouraged and challenged by loving leaders.

one

Look Out: Outreach

If the primary purpose of your Coffee Break program is outreach, then each Coffee Break leader must develop an outreach mindset. This may not come naturally to all leaders, but it can be developed over time. The following are key components to developing an outreach mindset.

The Foundation of Prayer

The entire Coffee Break ministry must rest on the foundation of prayer. The importance of prayer cannot be overemphasized. Make all of your decisions—from choosing your leaders to scheduling—only after praying earnestly about them. Begin praying for the unsaved people who will attend before you even begin promoting your program. If you start with prayer, you can be confident of God's leading, no matter how he guides your program.

Knowing Your Group Members

Depending on where you live, where your church is located, and where you advertise, the Lord may bring people very much like yourself into your program. However, he may also choose to give you a group of people with whom you have little in common. Trust that God will bring the right people to your group. If you were raised in a church setting and live where you mingle only with believers, this may be a new experience for you. You may be surprised at the language, the skepticism, or the lifestyle choices of your group members. Lost people don't always live by Christian values.

In that context you must refrain from being judgmental or argumentative. It is often better to wait until you are asked about controversial subjects than to raise them. Establish a climate that allows for disagreement but that also encourages people to listen to the biblical perspective. Always respond positively when your beliefs are challenged. Remember that what the Bible tells us about Christian living is based on God's love for us. Do not feel that you must have an answer for every question. You may be able to find out the answer, or you may have to admit that there are no answers to some questions.

If you have a number of people in your group who are not Christians and have little understanding of the Christian faith, consider using a number of lessons in the *Inspirit* series. *Inspirit: Real Answers for Real People* is a line of studies designed for people who have little or no church background. The material deals with practical life issues and offers an opportunity to ask questions and to find answers in the Bible. For more information about *Inspirit* resources, call CRC Publications (1-800-333-8300).

Building Relationships

Simply having a positive Coffee Break experience during the meeting time may not be enough to develop good relationships between you and your group members. Make contact with group members personally or by phone between meetings to build relationships with them. These may be informal get-togethers, such as meeting for lunch or going to a concert or sporting event. Send them a card, offer to take care of their children, bring them food if there is illness in the family, and so on. Don't be afraid to ask for their help or advice. They may have much to offer you too. Try to keep up the contact during breaks in your schedule.

Leading the Bible Study

In inductive Bible study, the truth does not flow from the leader to the group members; instead, the Bible is the teacher and the leader is a guide. As the Holy Spirit speaks through the Scriptures, leaders help group members hear the real message of the Bible. Your primary purpose is not to keep the discussion moving, but to guide the group into hearing what the Bible says.

More important than handling the mechanics of group discussion is your attitude as a leader. Do you clearly show respect for the Bible's authority? Can group members sense your love and openness to them? How much do you enjoy the discussion? Your attitude in these areas can make a real difference in the vitality and spirit of the group. However, your attitude toward the group cannot be developed by following certain guidelines. It must be molded by the Holy Spirit's work in your heart. This is why leaders are encouraged to pray for sensitivity, wisdom, and love.

One Coffee Break member observed an effective leader in the program in her church in Lacombe, Alberta. Here's what she saw:

> "She actually said (and did) very little [in the group]—except a body language that leaned forward to people as they spoke, eyes that listened and loved, and responses to questions that never said 'you're wrong,' but 'I see the Bible as saying this.' In a nutshell, she *loves,* and she does not live by the law, but by grace."

If possible, non-Christians should not be placed in groups composed of mostly Christians. Many Christians do not relate sensitively to non-Christians and sometimes inadvertently offend or threaten those not familiar with the Christian faith. In a group comprised of people having a variety of experience and biblical knowledge, non-Christians will be less likely to feel pressured or offended by insensitive attitudes or confused by theological jargon. They will probably feel more comfortable and free to express their thoughts, questions, and doubts. It will be important for those who have extensive biblical knowledge to relate sensitively to those in the group who do not.

Some of the mechanics of leading a discussion group will be covered in later sections of this manual.

Presenting the Gospel

Evangelism is a process, not an event. Life-change doesn't happen overnight. It is in an atmosphere of love that non-Christians can find a personal relationship with God. In time, they will begin to ask questions and understand more of what it means to be a Christian.

Often group members will give signs that they would like to hear more about salvation. They may ask pertinent questions; they may demonstrate a deeper interest in the lesson material. An alert leader will notice this personal interest during the discussion. A member who has been excited and responsive in the group may signal "the right time" by becoming quiet and thoughtful. Or the person who has been quiet, cautious, and even defensive may begin to respond more positively. A group member who becomes argumentative and belligerent may be showing signs of her internal struggle. Concerned leaders will be sensitive to these changes and depend on a God-given blend of boldness and sensitivity, along with a prayerful dependence on the Spirit's leading.

If members of your group begin asking questions about the gospel, you may want to explain the good news briefly in the group, and then spend time alone with the individual who asked the question. If they use word pictures to describe their situation, you may want to use those same word pictures in your explanation. For example, if they feel lost, or abandoned, or drowning, you could tell them about the one who finds them or who rescues them.

Each leader must be prepared to explain the hope they have within them (1 Pet. 3:15). Your personal testimony can be very effective in helping others. If you can relate your personal salvation experience, do so in simple words; people cannot respond to something they don't understand. Don't expect people to listen to a rambling, unorganized, or lengthy gospel presentation. Be sure to avoid using religious jargon that people may not understand, such as "sanctification," "redemption," "atonement," and so on.

If you need help preparing your testimony, see Carol Kent's book *Speak Up With Confidence,* especially chapter 10, "Your Life Story Has Potential! Preparing Your Personal Testimony" (Thomas Nelson Publishers, 1987). CRC Publications (1-800-333-8300) and Christian bookstores offer many resources. You will do best by using your own words. An easy way to remember the main points is simply A-B-C: *A—Admit that you are a sinner in need of a Savior.* **B**—*Believe that Jesus is the Savior who came into this world and died on the cross to pay for your sins.* **C**—*Commit yourself to living with thankfulness for all that God has done for you.* You can elaborate on the main points, but remember to keep it simple. Such a presentation must not be wooden or stilted; adapt it to your own personality and thoughts. Be prepared; practice giving your testimony to your Christian friends. As you gain experience you will feel more comfortable doing this.

The Growth Process

A person who has accepted Jesus as Savior will soon begin to grow spiritually. This requires nurture, training, discipline, and love. Good follow-up by mature Christians provides the context for spiritual growth.

Just as we must be sensitive in our approach to non-Christians, so too our follow-up must be done with sensitivity. New Christians are not imme-diately free from all defensiveness and ready to accept the lordship of Christ in every area of their lives. Growth takes time, and the rate of growth is different with each individual. We must remember that just as the new birth is the work of God, so also is spiritual growth. Good follow-up provides the contact and conditions that will stimulate growth. We can do much damage by forcing our patterns of Christian behavior on others. Let the Spirit and the Word lead the way in the new Christian's life, and be ready to follow with your sensitive guidance and support.

Spiritual growth for the new believer often takes place in the context of the Coffee Break group. Being part of a group enables new believers to experience being part of Christ's body. In a group setting the new believer learns how to live in Christ, to be rooted and built up in him, and to be established in the faith (Col. 2:6-7), as well as how to handle temptations and sin. The small group provides a place for new believers to share their weaknesses without being judged, a place where they are accepted as they are. The Coffee Break group also provides prayer support and offers a context in which new believers can learn to pray. New believers can look to the group for accountability and input on decisions they need to make, and the group can help them to discover and use their spiritual gifts. As new believers experience the excitement of knowing Jesus, they are more attuned to the lost people around them. Soon they are inviting others to learn more about Jesus!

People who have made a commitment to Jesus as Savior will often need one-on-one time with a leader. Many new believers experience a new awareness of sin and need to be reminded of God's forgiveness. They will experience doubts as Satan tempts them with old habits. It is critical that new believers have frequent personal contact with other believers who will remind them of God's promises and his love. New believers must be led to see their personal struggles in light of God's Word. They must take responsibility for sin and make changes in their lives. Gradually their lives will be transformed.

If new converts are already members of other Christian churches, do not pressure them to become members of your own. Rather, encourage them to be faithful, vital members of their own churches, while at the same time letting them know they are welcome at your church. Some may want to leave their church because it does not meet their spiritual needs but cannot do so for family reasons. Encourage them without discrediting their church or their family members. If their spiritual needs are not being met in their church, offer them as many opportunities for spiritual growth and fellowship as are possible in your church. They may benefit from being part of another small group at your church.

If new converts are not active in a church, invite them to your worship services, serving as a bridge between them and your church. Pick them up for services or meet them at the church to help them feel welcomed. It is important that church members accept new believers unconditionally. In love and grace new believers will be nurtured to become faithful followers of Jesus.

two

DECISIONS, DECISIONS: HOW TO GET STARTED

As you consider whether to begin a Coffee Break program, you will face many decisions. If you are starting to lead for the first time in an established program, this material is for you too, for it will help you better understand why your leaders do what they do.

Pray consistently and specifically for God's leading and the Holy Spirit's power. Without the work of the Spirit you will not have an effective Coffee Break program. If you have prayed, you will be at peace because you know that you are trying to follow God's leading.

Defining Your Purpose

Keeping the purpose clearly focused on evangelism will give clarity to your decisions. Your advertising, organizing, and activities will stem from your purpose, and your purpose will, in turn, be shaped by the Lord's leading as you pray.

1. Who is your target audience? Women? Men? A mixed group? Is it important to reach children through Story Hour and Little Lambs?

2. What timeframe will work best? Morning? Evening? After work hours? Saturday mornings? Keep all your options open, but realize that this

will be determined in part by the availability of your leaders. Leaders and group members often are willing to schedule work and other activities around Coffee Break once they realize its value.

3. Will this be a church-based program? If so, will you hold your meetings in a church building? In homes? Restaurants? Somewhere else? If this is a home-based program, how will this affect the rest of your family?

4. What format should you follow? How will you schedule your time together? Should you plan for a whole year of ministry, or give it a try for six or eight weeks?

5. Which Bible study guides will you use?

The Beginning Stages

Once you have discussed your options and made initial decisions, you will have to decide how to implement them and then take the next steps. This is often an exciting time in the life of the ministry.

1. Pray for leaders who love the Lord, who love the lost, and who love God's Word. God will raise up leaders to do his work. Don't try to talk people into leading. Leaders do not have to be Bible scholars, but some Bible background is helpful. They must be willing to give several hours in preparation for this ministry. Although it can be a very time-consuming and emotionally draining ministry, the rewards are incredible.

2. Plan for two leaders for each group of eight to twelve participants. There should be no more than twelve participants per group. Though sometimes groups are larger than twelve, participation by all the members generally declines in larger groups. If you have leaders available, divide the large group into two smaller ones. Groups do not have to be large in order to be effective, nor do you need many groups to have a successful program. Some programs do not grow in numbers as people move in and out of their programs. Do not measure your success by numbers. Your job is to be faithful to God's calling and to let the Holy Spirit work.

3. Develop a good working relationship with other leaders and staff. If you start a Story Hour or Little Lambs program for preschoolers and toddlers, be sure that the leaders of all programs communicate regularly and that all leaders are equally involved in decision-making. If you have a nursery, prayer partners, kitchen help, or any other support staff, make sure to develop a good relationship with them from the start. Remember that each individual ministry is of equal importance and that each person involved in the ministry is important. Remember, too, that children need consistency; having the same leaders each week is important to them. Your whole program will benefit if you work side-by-side in planning.

4. Train your leaders. It is frustrating to be asked to serve in a ministry for which you have no preparation. Training workshops are available in most regions of the United States and Canada. Regional representatives are available for phone consultation if you are too far from the nearest workshop. Call 1-888-644-0814 for the name of the regional representative nearest you. This manual is a good foundation for those who are unable to attend a training workshop. It is also helpful to observe another Coffee Break program. Your regional representative can help you make contact with leaders of a nearby program.

5. Determine your budget. Coffee Break is a relatively inexpensive program to operate. The leader and Bible study guides are necessary, but worth the small expense. Providing snacks and drinks sets a warm, inviting atmosphere, so you will probably want to invest in those. You can suggest a donation basket for participants to help defray expenses. Those who come to the group will often want to participate by bringing treats; in fact, if you offer a sign-up sheet, they are likely to show up on those dates for which they've volunteered. Participating in supplying treats also helps members feel ownership of the group and gives them a way to show their gratitude. (Be sure to model that a store-purchased snack has as much value as a home-baked goodie.) Remember to include in your budget the cost of leadership training, childcare (if necessary), study materials, and promotion. You may also want to include expenses for sending your leaders to the biennial Coffee Break convention for expanded leadership training and inspiration.

6. Plan your promotion. Remember that your purpose is reaching the lost with the good news of Jesus Christ. Where will you find the lost? Pray for them, and you will be led to them. Open your eyes for opportunities to give out an invitation to natural contacts, such as neighbors, friends, coworkers, children's parents, hairdressers, librarians, and so on. Pray for eyes to see the doors God opens to you. It's often easier if you have a brief written invitation to give people, so they will have a reminder of the date, place, and time. Word-of-mouth is by far the most effective advertising strategy. As is true in the business world, satisfied customers spread the word. Don't be discouraged if your initial response is small. Some other promotion options are telephone book advertising, newspaper ads, church signs, and flyers at grocery stores, Laundromats, nursery schools, and homeless shelters.

   What should you include in your advertising? Think about what information you would want to know if you were receiving the invitation. You would want an address, directions, and information about which door to enter, what to bring, and what time the event begins and ends. People will also want to know about the availability of childcare and whether casual dress is appropriate. You may include phrases to reassure newcomers to Bible study (for example, "no experience necessary" or "no previous Bible knowledge needed"). If you plan to give Bibles to those who come, you may want to mention that fact. If there is another church in your area doing a similar ministry, perhaps you can advertise together. Churches with similar programs should always be thinking and working cooperatively, not competitively. Call CRC Publications (1-800-333-8300) for information on flyers and logos that can be adapted for use in your local setting.

   If you want people to register ahead of time, you may want them to telephone someone who is home often, or give the hours when a church secretary could be reached. A friendly voice on the phone can be encouraging. If you offer a personal invitation, also offer to pick them up or meet them at the door the first time. That assures them that they will not have to enter a strange building alone.

7. Schedule your ministry year. However, remember that a newcomer may be intimidated to see a calendar for an entire year at the first meeting.

18

Perhaps you could schedule your first six weeks or so and let group members know that you plan to continue after that. When planning your schedule, be sure to consider school vacations, holidays, and the number of lessons in your study materials. Most group members depend on the weekly Bible study for spiritual nourishment and do not want meetings suspended or spaced too far apart. The desire for regular and continued Bible study is often so strong that some churches offer sessions in the summer. If you do so, make sure that your leaders get any breaks they need.

8. Plan your study materials. CRC Publications has developed a series of inductive Bible studies prepared especially for the Coffee Break ministry. Call 1-800-333-8300 for a free CRC Publications catalog, or view the catalog on-line at www.crcpublications.org. Many different studies, based on both Old and New Testament books, are available in three formats.

   - **Discover Your Bible.** These Bible studies are based on a book of the Bible or on a selected biblical theme. They assume some advance preparation by the group member. The CRC Publications catalog ranks the studies "basic," "intermediate," or "advanced" so that you can choose materials that are appropriate for your group.
   - **Discover Life.** These studies are topical. For each session, the passage to be studied and the discussion questions are printed on the study page. These studies do not assume advance preparation by the group member; however, the topical nature of the studies generates good discussion. These studies also are ranked "basic," "intermediate," or "advanced."
   - **Inspirit.** These topical study guides are entry-level. They assume no previous Bible knowledge. They are written to help people see that the Bible does have answers to life's questions and are well suited for people who may not be interested in a Bible study group, but who want to study a certain topic.

   CRC Publications develops new studies and revises the older material. Your suggestions are always welcome. If you have questions about what to order, call a customer service representative at CRC Publications or your regional representative. While it is helpful for newcomers to Bible study to begin with the start of a narrative, most people seem to adapt well whenever they join. If you plan to study one of the gospels every other year, you will ensure that new group members "meet Jesus" fairly soon in their Bible study experience. Mark seems to be the easiest of the gospels. Other short studies from the Discover Your Bible series that work especially well for beginners are Ruth, Esther, and Jonah.

9. If you are working in a church-based program, develop a supportive relationship between your Coffee Break ministry and the rest of the congregation. Your pastor should be visible, though remain in the background. The pastor may want to pick up a cup of coffee occasionally or be introduced by the leaders, but the pastor's primary role is support and encouragement. Many congregations are not used to providing ministries whose primary target group is outside the membership of the church. You will have to explain your mission carefully, so that everyone understands what you are attempting to do. The congregation should be encouraged to pray for the Coffee Break ministry and will be asked to support it financially through the church budget.

    You may want to invite some people from your congregation who are "on the fringe" of congregational life; however, ordinarily don't issue a "blanket invitation" for anyone interested to attend. If there is a need for Bible study among your church members, you may want to offer another time slot during which the church members would be invited to study the same material. Don't underestimate the difficulty of these policies. Give careful thought to your explanations.

10. Plan to evaluate your program periodically. Periodic informal evaluating will be done in the leaders' meeting throughout the year, but you should also plan to go through a more formal evaluation at the end of the year. Think about the different facets of your ministry and ask if anything could be improved. Ask if life-change is happening to group members. Do they seem to be learning? To focus your discussion, ask how the group can become so valuable to people that they will be willing to change their schedule to be a part of it.

11. Plan now for dropouts. Sometimes people will attend once in order to try out your group. You may find that they are already believers or that your study does not meet their needs. You may want to contact them and wish them well or give some suggestions about other studies that may be available. Others may not return for unknown reasons; they should be contacted by a leader or group member. Gently ask them to tell you honestly why they are not returning. Learn from your mistakes; make any necessary changes from their suggestions. Without pressuring them, let them know that you miss them in the group. At the beginning of a new season or a new book send them an invitation to let them know that you're still thinking about them and that they are always welcome. But be sensitive to the fact that some people prefer to be left alone. Continue to pray for those who drop out. Do not blame yourself. It may be their personal preference to leave the group; small groups are not for everyone.

12. Decide whether you want to plan any social events as a group. The agenda for these events should be nonthreatening, entertaining, and socially interactive. These events may be used as an opportunity for group members to invite their friends. Group members may enjoy being involved in the planning and preparing. Social events are a great way to show non-Christians how much fun Christians can have.

13. Some church-based groups include a singing time as part of their opening or closing activities. Because we attend church, we believers are not put off by singing. But singing with others is not a familiar part of our contemporary world, so many non-Christians are not likely to be comfortable singing. Singing together may have the effect of singling out the non-Christians. We also don't want people to sing words that are not true for them, or words that they don't understand.

On the other hand, singing is a way for Christians to worship God, and it is a good way for non-Christians to experience the love that we have for God. It is also a way for them to become acquainted with some beautiful Christian music. Whether or not you have musicians and worship leaders will also influence your decision. You may want to play a Christian CD occasionally to let your group have a taste of Christian music, if you choose not to sing.

14. A nursery can be a tremendous asset to a daytime program. It is best to have at least one mature, qualified person as a permanent nursery supervisor, a person the children recognize and trust each time they come. Young children need continuity from week to week. Other volunteers can take turns as nursery helpers.

It is worth the extra effort to have child care available. Many mothers have acknowledged that they came to Coffee Break initially because of the free nursery, coffee, and adult conversation. As they studied the Bible, they found that it changed their lives. They came to receive a break from their routine, but they left with a far greater blessing.

The Initial Meeting

Plan your get-acquainted meeting. Some groups invite special speakers to draw more people. Gauge your community; if you think a special speaker, demonstration, or other drawing card would help, try it. Other groups spend their first time together getting to know each other. You could plan some icebreaker games or ask a few questions to get conversations started.

Whatever you do, you'll want to give a warm welcome. If there's any question about which door should be used, post a big sign, hang balloons, or station a greeter in the parking lot. Offer food and a relaxed atmosphere. Have name tags ready right away so people can get to know each other. Make sure the leaders are completely ready before the starting time so that they are available to talk with all the guests. Dress casually to reflect the low-key atmosphere you want to establish.

One of the leaders should take this opportunity to inform newcomers about the Bible study. Sometime during your first get-together you'll probably want to

- Introduce all the leaders.
- Distribute study guides, perhaps giving a very brief overview or other introduction. Encourage people to answer the questions in advance, but also encourage them to come and participate even if they haven't completed their lesson.
- If you have a Story Hour, Little Lambs, or oth r child care program, introduce a leader to give some information or guidelines for that program.

- Invite people to ask friends who may be interested. Have extra flyers about the program to give them.
- Set the tone for the group discussions. Assure people that they will not be put on the spot, that they will have the freedom to enter the discussion as they feel comfortable. Encourage them to ask questions. Tell them they are not expected to have any previous Bible knowledge or to know the answers. Explain the role of the leader as a discussion guide, not a teacher. Emphasize that the Bible contains the answers. You might also note that denominational differences will not be discussed and that you will concentrate on discovering together what the Bible says.
- If you have Bibles to give away, tell people where they are and that they can pick one up on their way out. You may want to mark the passage you intend to discuss at the first Bible study with a slip of paper or bookmark.
- Tell them anything they need to know about coffee and refreshments. If they will be taking turns providing a treat, make sure you have some store-bought goodies the first time so that they see that as an option.

three

FOLLOW THE LEADER: DEVELOPING YOUR LEADERSHIP STAFF

Qualities of the Leader

Coffee Break leaders must love the Lord. They must love God's Word. They must be interested in reaching the lost. Some of those qualities are developed as a leader begins to study with a group of leaders and becomes more mature in the faith. Leaders must have time available: time to prepare, time to lead, and time to reach group members outside of group time. Leaders must be sensitive to the lost and willing to learn. They must be reliable in carrying out their responsibilities. Leaders should also be people of prayer. They must pray for the program, for their coleaders, and for their group members.

Leaders do not need to be Bible experts. They will learn all they need to know about the passage under study as they prepare from week to week. It is helpful, but not necessary, to be familiar with the rest of the Bible. It is important that the leader be able to convey information without sounding like a teacher. The leader must be a guide in the conversation, helping the group members discover for themselves what the Bible says.

Leaders do not have to be sinless. They must acknowledge their sin and seek forgiveness. They should also realize that their lives may be under scrutiny. The apostle Paul, in 1 Thessalonians, urged his followers to imitate his life. A leader should live a life that is worthy of being followed—an awesome responsibility! The life of the leader should, like Paul's, imitate the life of Jesus Christ.

Leaders should be people of compassion, people who are ready to listen. They should not expect Christian behavior from nonbelievers. At the same time, a leader must know the truths of God's Word.

Job Description

Let's be honest here. Investing in people's lives takes time, so leading Coffee Break takes time. If you meet weekly, you'll need to figure on investing five to seven hours to do the work well. You will need more than an hour to prepare your lesson on your own. You will need one to two hours for the leaders' meeting. You will need more than two hours when your group meets (for setting up and cleaning up, as well as leading the group).

Being a Coffee Break leader also means spending time with your group members outside of the group. You may meet for coffee, breakfast, or lunch. You may spend time on the phone. You must be available to handle emergencies. That being said, you will have to learn how to balance your ministry and your personal life.

Although it can be time-consuming, Coffee Break is also an incredibly rewarding ministry. Nothing is more exciting than leading someone into a personal relationship with Jesus Christ. Guiding group members along the way as they become more open to the claims of the gospel and watching them develop to spiritual maturity once they've made a commitment is an exciting process. Plus, as a leader you will grow tremendously. You will gain confidence in leading groups, in serving others, in reaching the lost, and in other areas that will carry over into other parts of your life. Most Coffee Break leaders find that being a leader is an integral part of their own spiritual growth. Yes, you must give a lot; but you also receive a lot in return.

Different Leader Roles

Flexibility is the key to a good leadership relationship. Leaders may play various roles at different times in their lives. These should be based on the spiritual gifts that God has given to them.

1. Some leaders will want to lead every session. They may want to have an assistant leader who can help them by
   - Developing relationships with group members.
   - Supporting the leader during the meeting, such as rephrasing the question after a long silence.
   - Catching background comments and body language that the leader may miss.
   - Assisting in making phone calls.
   - Supporting the leader apart from the group.
   - Providing constructive criticism when necessary.
   - Leading when necessary because of illness or scheduling conflicts.

2. Sometimes leaders may be training new leaders. In that case you will probably want to consider the new leader an apprentice leader. The apprentice leader would
   - Develop relationships with group members.
   - Be supportive of and mentored by the leader.
   - Catch background comments and body language that the leader may miss.
   - Assist in making phone calls.
   - Support the leader apart from the group.
   - Provide constructive criticism when necessary.
   - Gradually learn different aspects of leading the group. New leaders will acquire gradually the leadership skills necessary to lead the group if they try out one thing at a time. They might begin by asking an icebreaker question. Then, another time, they may try a question or two from the study guide. They may take prayer requests, pray, and so on, until they have learned how to do each part of leading the group. At that point the apprentice can begin to do several of the tasks at a time, until the apprentice is well prepared to lead his or her own group.

   Be careful not to push apprentice leaders too fast into leadership. Some people do not have the gifts to be leaders, and as they realize that, they may find other ways to serve. It is natural for new leaders to be nervous at first, but if that nervousness is intense and continues for many weeks, it may be better for them to find another way to minister.

3. There are other ways in which people can help serve in Coffee Break—for example, as greeters, set-up or clean-up people, coffee servers, transportation providers, party planners, and so on. Don't be afraid to try to get group members involved in some of these tasks as the year progresses. The more they are involved in the ministry, the more likely they will stay and feel valued. The more group members are involved, the more they consider the group "their group," and that will benefit everyone.

Training for Ministry

Regional representatives are available throughout the year to train Coffee Break leaders. Many training sessions are scheduled in the fall. Contact your representative to find out about upcoming events. The training covers many of the topics that are found in this book, but in an interactive, hands-on way. At the training session you will have opportunity to talk with leaders from other programs in your area, which may turn into a great networking service. Training workshops for leading Story Hour and Little Lambs are also available. All leaders benefit from workshops, even those who have worked in other Bible study programs or in other churches. Your pastor may also want to attend the workshop in order to better understand your program. The workshop fees are reasonable and often are paid by the churches of those who attend. You can find out about workshops in your area by calling 1-888-644-0814.

In the event that some of your prospective leaders are unable to attend a training workshop, you should set aside some time to study the material in this guide together. If possible, visit another Coffee Break program in your area.

How to Stay Connected

If you are a Coffee Break leader, you should let your regional representative know, so that your name can be added to the *Connections* mailing list. *Connections* is a quarterly publication that addresses small group and children's ministries, particularly Coffee Break, Story Hour, and Little Lambs. You can read *Connections* for ideas, inspiration, and information about these ministries. You can also have your name added to the mailing list by calling 1-888-644-0814.

In alternating years a Coffee Break convention is held. These conventions are attended by Coffee Break, Story Hour, and Little Lambs leaders and support staff from throughout Canada and the United States. The purpose of the Coffee Break convention is to inspire and educate leaders in their ministries by means of speakers, worship, and sectionals. Hundreds of program leaders will attest to the value of the conventions. Registration information is conveyed via the *Connections* newsletter.

Leaders' Meetings

Leaders' meetings can be the glue that holds your Coffee Break program together. It is here that leaders bond together through the Word and through prayer. Here they find the strength to stretch beyond their comfort zone and unite in the purpose of outreach. Here leaders laugh together, cry together, pray together, and work together. This time provides personal growth as well as preparation to lead a group. As much as possible, encourage nursery, Story Hour, and Little Lambs leaders to participate too.

In some churches, leaders' meetings are so important that if the leaders don't attend the meeting, they may not lead that lesson. The leaders' meeting is a time for your leaders to meet together to pray for your ministry, to plan for the future, and to prepare to lead the lesson.

In the leaders' meeting you will want to do the following:

- Pray for your ministry together and for your needs as a leader. Spend your time praying together rather than discussing prayer requests. Limit your prayers to those needs that affect your leaders' ministry in Coffee Break. Remember to hold prayer requests in confidence. Your fellow leaders may be your most powerful prayer warriors. Don't jeopardize this strategic confidential relationship.
- Plan for the future of your ministry together. You will need an eye on the past and an eye on the future. Evaluate briefly the success of the previous group lesson and encourage each other as leaders. Brainstorm ways to reach families and better minister to group members. Talk together about your fund-raisers, if necessary, and your convention plans. Think ahead to the next ministry season, and begin gathering

ideas to improve your program. Plan ways to celebrate your ministry together, by going out to dinner, for example.

- Prepare to lead your lesson. Each leader should be prepared for this meeting by studying individually first. Before the leaders' meeting, each leader should:

> Pray for insight.
>
> Read the entire passage to be covered in the lesson.
>
> Write answers in your own study guide, or underline them in the Bible. Remember that you should not take the leader guide to the group meeting.
>
> Write additional questions in your own study guide that will help group members understand the biblical material. Use complete sentences rather than phrases, so that you won't be fumbling for words as you lead.
>
> Read the leader guide for additional suggestions.
>
> Read any additional commentaries as needed. If some in your group use study Bibles, you may want to read those notes as well. Encourage your groups, however, not to shortchange their own discovery process. Read study Bible notes only after wrestling with the passage first.

If leaders have done this preparation on their own, your leaders' meeting should be a fruitful and enjoyable time together. Go through the lesson as a group of leaders just as you would in the group. If you take turns leading the questions you will develop your skills as a leader. Ask the questions you plan to ask in the group. Answer the questions the way you think your group members will. This will force your leaders to rephrase questions as they go along, a valuable skill in leading the group. Rarely does the group go through the questions just as written, so you should be prepared to think rapidly within the group setting.

Tips for Using Your Study Guide

- If you need more space for notes, remove the staples, insert paper, and restaple.
- Use different colors of ink for different kinds of questions.
- Use asterisks to highlight important questions.

- Use abbreviations for names or phrases you use often (e.g., Wdim=What does it mean . . . ?, JtB=John the Baptist).
- Write the times in your margins of when you need to start each section in order to finish the entire lesson on time.
- Write in the margin information gleaned from the leader guide so that you are aware of when you are "teaching" rather than guiding.

Don't underestimate the amount of spiritual growth that will happen to you as a leader! For many leaders, Coffee Break is an important vehicle to their own spiritual maturity. Being a Coffee Break leader encourages personal Bible study, prayer, accountability, caring, open-mindedness, sensitivity, focusing on the unsaved, church attendance, and learning to know other leaders on a deeper level.

Finally, *relax!* Remember that God does not call where he does not equip. Allow room for the Holy Spirit's leading. Recognize that growth in leadership is a process. Allow yourself the time to learn. If you prepare yourself responsibly, trust the results to God.

four

QUESTIONS, QUESTIONS, QUESTIONS: THE INDUCTIVE METHOD OF BIBLE STUDY

The word *inductive* describes a method of studying something. It involves looking at the details and then at the big picture, drawing conclusions based on what has been discovered. The leader in such a group uses questions as the primary method for guiding group members to discover the truths of God's Word for themselves. Group members work directly with a Bible passage, using questions designed to help them understand the passage. They do not immediately refer to a manual for help in interpreting the passage, or first read a book and then turn to the Bible for information. They do not use the Scripture passage simply as a springboard to launch into their own ideas. Instead, the inductive method requires them to put aside their preconceived notions and to come to the Bible with an open mind to discover what the Scripture says and means. The concept of discovery is so important to Coffee Break that the series of Bible study books designed for Coffee Break is called "Discover Your Bible." As leaders, we want to help people find out what the Bible has to say.

Why Use the Inductive Method?

- The inductive method honors God's Word. It recognizes the Bible as the inspired Word of God. It also takes into account the situations and personalities of the human authors God used to give his Word. Inductive study honors the Word by recognizing the significance of every part of a passage.
- The inductive method encourages personal study and insures that the individual's study will bear even more fruit when joined with the group's efforts. Using this method guarantees that the group will honestly grapple with the Scripture to discover its important truths.
- Inductive Bible study teaches an important discipline. This kind of Bible study requires time and effort. Learning to ask questions of the text is a discipline that most people will not forget. It will significantly change their understanding of the Bible. Learning this method offers tremendous potential for growth and development for each individual in the group. It is a method that enables group members to feed themselves with God's Word for a lifetime.
- Inductive Bible study encourages acceptance of the Word. People learn better when they discover a truth than when they are told one. This method invites people to see for themselves, and frequently turns doubters into believers. Being in contact with God's Word changes lives. Many have come to believe in Jesus as Savior through being part of a Coffee Break group. Many more have seen distinct changes in their lives as a result of studying God's Word on a regular basis.
- Inductive Bible study is exciting. Digging into God's Word develops an excitement that keeps Coffee Break members returning week after week, year after year. When people discover that the Bible is interesting and relevant to their needs and problems, they become excited about studying it. God's Word is powerful in changing lives, even more so when it is studied in a consistent and regular way.

Using Questions to Lead Your Group

In addition to prayer, the most beneficial way a leader can prepare is to plan good questions to ask in the group setting. Your group members will use study guides which present the primary discussion questions. Think of these questions as the skeleton on which the lesson will hang.

The leader's guide provides supplementary questions for the leader to ask in the group. Not all questions in the leader guide will be used in the group discussion. These supplementary questions are suggestions to the leader, who may or may not choose to use them. In the best of leaders' meetings the leaders will wrestle with the questions to develop even better ones, ones that reflect the personality of the group and of the leader.

Asking good questions comes naturally to some leaders, but all leaders can develop their skills in this area. The best way is to write down your own questions in response to the passage before you even read the leader's guide. Once you train yourself to continually ask questions of the text, you will find that question-writing becomes much easier. Writing good questions leads to asking good questions in the group, even when the discussion veers slightly from what was anticipated. If you have worked with the material in developing good questions, you will thoroughly understand the material and you will learn how to keep the discussion flowing through questions.

When writing questions, you can avoid some difficulties by anticipating the answers that group members might give. Determine whether the answer can be found in the text or if it depends on some prior knowledge that is not available to everyone in the group. If you can identify which verse answers your question, you probably have a question that can be answered by anyone in the group.

Ask open-ended questions that cannot be answered by a simple "yes" or "no." Questions that have several possible answers create a better discussion than do brief answers. Using several different kinds of questions will help to create a more open, sharing atmosphere in your group.

- Use an Opening Share Question as an icebreaker. Some of the leader guides in the Discover Your Bible series provide an Opening Share Question for each lesson. You could also make up your own share question. Make sure that it is a question everyone in the group can answer. This is a way of ensuring that everyone in the group has a chance to talk, which will make them more likely to speak up later during the discussion. These questions need not be related to the lesson, though it is a good challenge to try to make them so. If you were studying the story of Jesus and the Samaritan woman (John 4), for example, you could ask icebreaker questions such as "What's the thirstiest you've ever been?" or "Did you ever have to ask a stranger for help?"

- Make sure that the group gets the facts straight by using factual observation questions, for example, "Where did this story take place?" or "Where had the disciples gone?"
- Help people see the bigger picture by using interpretation questions. "What do you think the author is really saying?" or "How does Jesus move her from the physical to the spiritual?"
- Low-key application questions should be carefully phrased so that no one feels put on the spot. For example, ask, "How might someone apply this?" or, "What does this say to the twenty-first century?" or, "What does this passage tell us about how we ought to live today?" Use "we" and "us" rather than "you" to challenge the group without appearing judgmental or putting others on the spot. If you want to use a more pointed application question, consider using a "Traveling Question" designed to provoke some thought on the way home. For example, "How could I work on being more kind this week?"

Other Considerations for Leaders

While using commentaries for interpretation can provide valuable background information for the leader, be cautious in presenting such information to the group. You want to convey to the group that what they need to know is accessible to them in the passage itself. "Study" Bibles function in the same way that commentaries do. Suggest that the group look at the passage first and read the study helps only after the discussion. You may have to remind your group that "the top part is the Bible," lest they think the real truth can be found in the notes at the bottom of the Bible page.

Occasionally you may refer to another passage to clarify the one under discussion. This is valid, since the Bible is an integrated, unified book in which important biblical truths are repeated in a variety of ways and settings. This also helps the beginning Bible student learn of the Bible's unity and comprehensiveness. But there are many dangers in using other passages.

- First, doing so tends to set the leader apart as the teacher, making the rest of the group a class. This can dampen the spontaneity of the discussion. The real teacher is the Bible, and the leader is the person who guides the discussion.

- Second, using other passages may hinder the discovery principle by introducing extra material that the group has not been able to study before the meeting. Group members may be put in the position of becoming observers instead of discoverers by looking at what the leader has already discovered. A good leader will try to find a way to keep the excitement of discovery alive.
- Third, referring to other passages opens the door to misuse of the Scriptures. Texts can be misinterpreted when they are used out of context as isolated statements. We want our group members to learn to use passages correctly and in context. If you use additional passages, make sure that you note the context of the passage and show how it relates to the topic under discussion.

five

READY, SET, GO:
LEADING YOUR GROUP

A s you begin to lead your group, keep these things in mind:
- Seat the group in a close, informal circle. Sitting around a table is the best arrangement because it emphasizes the need to study and write. Be certain that each person can see everyone else in the group. There should be no second row of seats.
- Get started on time. Complete your own preparation well before the starting time and begin promptly even if there are latecomers. The subtle pressure of knowing that the group consistently starts on time is the best way to cure people of arriving late.
- Make sure that everyone in the group is introduced to the others. Wear nametags until everyone knows each other's name well. Make sure that the group always wears nametags when you have visitors or new-comers. Introduce newcomers, but be sensitive to the person who wants to remain in the background.
- Let the group members read the passage. This is one way to begin to get individual members involved. Read a section at a time, and break longer sections into smaller paragraphs. Remember that there are those who would rather not read aloud because of a reading disability, poor

eyesight, a speech impediment, or shyness. You can ask, "Who wants to read first?" or, "Would somebody read this next section?" This is a good time to "read" your group members' body language. Someone may be hesitant to volunteer, but if she is making eye contact and her body language is leaning forward in anticipation it is fine to ask her by name to read.

Get the discussion started. Remember that your excitement and anticipation will be contagious. A number of methods can help you get started:

- Ask an icebreaker question. That's a fun way to get the discussion started, and usually many group members will participate. It's also often a time of laughter, which gets the discussion started on the right foot.
- Review the high points of the previous lesson in order to set the tone and orient the group to the passage.
- Preview the current lesson to build anticipation. Don't be afraid of occasionally expressing your own feelings about the lesson: "I really liked this lesson" or "I thought this was a difficult lesson."
- Relate the passage to major themes of the biblical book you are studying. Show how the section you are studying relates to preceding or following passages.
- Use a map, if it will be helpful, to trace journeys or find cities.

Keep the group atmosphere low-key and conducive to navigating group members through the lesson.

- A warm and relaxed atmosphere of acceptance encourages freedom in sharing, learning, and responding. A touch of humor helps the group relax. Try to be relaxed yourself. If you find that you are very nervous, a humorous remark about it may help you and the group not to take it too seriously. The leader who increasingly rests in the Lord will find it possible to experience and communicate both enthusiasm and the calmness that will make the group feel comfortable.
- Although you should not be heavy-handed in guiding the discussion, you must be able to control and redirect the thoughts of group members who try to monopolize or sidetrack the discussion. Be sure that no one is belittled or embarrassed and that everyone is given a fair

hearing. This must be done lovingly and tactfully. Always remember that during the discussion the good of the group is of more concern than that of the individual. You can follow through with an individual later. The group will become increasingly relaxed as it gains confidence in the leader who exercises this kind of loving leadership.

- While the Holy Spirit may press individual group members, try to keep the group discussion low-key (you will want to follow up with individuals who demonstrate a need for one-on-one discussion). Keep spiritual sharing at a low emotional level. Keep the emotional climate relaxed and informal. Though group members should feel free to express their feelings openly, your job is to ensure the comfort of all the members.

- Point out the table of contents in the front of the Bible so that group members can use it to find the Scripture passages. Tell them that the larger numbers in the Bible are chapter numbers and that the smaller numbers are the verses. Make sure to point out which question you're working on, especially as you move from one question to another, as most of the questions you ask won't appear in their books.

- Keep the discussion clear. As the leader, you must have a good grasp of the essential truths of the lesson. Correct obvious errors gently, if such errors will hurt the group's understanding, but don't feel that you have to correct every misstatement. Doing so may place both you and the group on the defensive. Let the Bible speak for itself. For example, say, "There is a verse in the Bible that speaks to that issue, Val. Let me tell you what it says there." See that unclear words and contributions are clarified. Ask, "Could you explain what you mean by that?" or, "Could you give an example of how that works out?"

- Use language that is clearly understood. Occasionally, you may need to explain the customs of Bible times. Don't use "Bible lingo," that is, words like *justification* and *redemption.* If you use words such as *Christian, grace,* or *faith,* explain what they mean. For example, "By Christian I mean someone who has a personal relationship with Jesus Christ." You want to foster the attitude that the Bible is both authoritative and understandable. The glossary of terms found in each leader guide and study guide will be a helpful resource for your group members. Use it regularly as you work through the lessons.

- Regulate the pace of the lessons and keep the discussion moving. Don't remain on any one point so long that people grow weary of it. Remember that the good of the group is more important than that of the individual. We're whetting their appetites, not exhausting the material. Ordinarily you should be able to cover a lesson each time you get together. If you have trouble finishing, try writing the time in the margin next to where you want to be at certain times.
- Conclude the discussion with questions or statements that summarize the main points of the lesson. Be sure to focus on the Bible rather than opinions here. The objective is to fix the main ideas firmly in the minds of the group members. End on time, even if you have to break off mid-sentence. Those who want to continue the discussion can stay after the meeting for a few minutes. It is important to honor others' time commitments, especially those of childcare helpers or Story Hour and Little Lambs leaders.

Establish rapport with the group by making sure there is an even give-and-take in the conversational flow. Your eye contact and body language will encourage group members to participate in the discussion.

- You occasionally may want to look at your book after asking a question and wait to see who begins to answer before looking up. Allow plenty of time for a response after you ask a question. People often need time to think and reflect. If there is no answer, explain or rephrase the question, or divide it into parts, but do not answer it yourself. You may be uncomfortable with silence at first, but you will soon relax as you realize its value.
- Use group members' names in discussion. For example, say, "Sue brought up a good point a while ago. How does what she said fit in here?" Usually you will not need to call on people; they will volunteer answers.
- Tie loose ends together as you proceed through the lesson. Summarize and rephrase on occasion, but not every time someone answers. Occasionally ask whether anyone has questions. Respond to their nonverbal messages, too, asking, for example, "Maria, you look puzzled," or "Gerry, you look like you have an idea."

- Always remember that you are a guide, not a teacher. Avoid using the words *teacher* and *class*. Bring in background information only when necessary to clarify the passage. Encourage group members to stay with the passage being discussed. It becomes confusing when too much extra material is brought into the discussion.
- Refer comments or questions from individuals back to the group: "That's a good question, Lois. What would the rest of you say about that?" You will find the principle of synergism at work here—the group as a whole will usually learn more from discussing the passage together than any of the members would learn individually.

Don't underestimate the power of prayer within the group. People are drawn to a group that takes prayer seriously. It may take them a while to suggest a prayer request, but they learn much by listening to how you pray and what you ask of God.

- Be careful not to "box God in" when you pray in your group. Ask for healing, for example, but also ask for the grace to cope if healing is not God's will.
- You want your group members to begin to pray on their own at home, so don't be too wordy or flashy in your prayers. Keep your prayers simple.
- Occasionally you may want to thank God for some aspect of his character that was revealed in the lesson. Or you may ask God to make you more like someone in the lesson. But resist moralizing. It is most important to show your group what a relationship with our heavenly Father is like.
- If you write prayer requests on blank pages in your study guide, you will model for your group the practice of keeping track of what you've prayed for and also that God answers prayer. You may want to follow up on earlier requests and note how God answered your prayers, thanking him.
- Be firm on issues of confidentiality. Be sure that each member of the group realizes the importance of keeping strict confidentiality. Only in cases of abuse, suicide, or homicide should there be any question of sharing information outside the group. Then it is best to ask the person involved for permission to tell someone else.

Be prepared to keep simple records.

- You'll want an address and phone number for each group member so that you can contact group members between sessions or in case of emergency. Some groups like to share the registration information by way of a phone list. Be sure to ask for permission; someone may have an unpublished phone number that should not be circulated.
- You may also make up a sign-up sheet for bringing treats if you've decided to do that.
- It's helpful to track attendance so that you can notice trends through the years. If attendance drops significantly at certain times, perhaps you need to schedule a break.
- Keep a record from year to year of who the leaders are and what you study. You may think that you will never forget, but over the years you might.

As your attendance grows, you will have to address the question of how to divide the people into groups.

- Generally you will want to group together those who are new to Bible study. If you were attending a computer class and knew nothing about computers, you'd want to be in a group of people with similar knowledge. If you think the discussion will be too stilted, consider including one or two sensitive believers who will be able to add to the discussion.
- It can be difficult to determine how familiar someone is with the Bible. Ask questions such as "Are you new to Bible study?" or "What experience have you had in Bible study?" Don't assume too much from a statement about church affiliation.
- Try to keep your group under twelve in number. If you have twelve or more, you will find that some will not talk much at all. Even Jesus had only twelve in his small group!
- Plan for growth. Keep your eyes open for new leaders. Invite your group members to ask friends to join you. Send a few extra invitations when you contact those who were part of your program during the previous season. Ask them to invite friends. Ask church members and your pastor for names of people you could contact.

six

WHAT NOW? CHALLENGES IN LEADING THE GROUP

A s with any kind of small group effort, Coffee Break can be a difficult, messy ministry. There are often no clear-cut answers to important leadership questions. But by keeping three simple principles in mind you will be able to face most any challenge ahead:

1. The goal of Coffee Break is to reach the lost.

2. While leaders must be sensitive to the needs and feelings of each person, the good of the group must take precedence over that of the individual.

3. The Bible is the focus of attention.

How do we deal with people who don't prepare their lessons ahead of time? Many people realize that they will learn more if they put in a bit of effort before the group meets, but even those who don't prepare can learn something. When you are reading the passage in your group, therefore, remember that this is the first time some of your group members will have read the passage. Give people time to absorb the words, and ask questions to clarify the basic ideas. Often it is a group member who sets the example of working through the lesson ahead of time. Once others try it, they often find they like the study better and learn more from it. So encourage your group members to do their lessons before coming to the session, but also encourage them to come and participate even if they don't have their lessons finished.

How do we deal with latecomers? Welcome them with a smile or brief greeting. Allow room for them to blend in with as little disruption to the group as possible. Don't review what you have covered, as that may set a pattern for more tardiness. Say which question you are discussing and move on.

What do we do when we have a low turnout? Don't apologize; focus instead on those who are there. Be courteous to them by starting on time. Take advantage of the smaller group, perhaps rearranging the chairs into a cozier setting. Good discussions often happen when the group is small and group dynamics allow for greater intimacy.

What if I ask a question and no one answers? Wait. It is most difficult for the leader to judge the silence. The group may be thinking, rereading the passage, or trying to find an answer in their books. If you have another leader in your group, it may work well to let them break the silence, perhaps rephrasing the question for you, such as, "Are you asking . . .?" If you are leading alone, ask, "Too easy? Too hard?" That may elicit a response, and you will know what kind of follow-up question to ask. Usually it is better not to answer the question yourself, lest you set up an awkward pattern.

How do we deal with denominational differences? The leader's role is to keep the discussion focused on what the Bible says. In general you will emphasize commonalities, not differences. Rarely do denominational teachings have to be part of the discussion. When it seems that these kinds of questions could arise, it is best to handle them yourself as you start the discussion. For example, if you are studying the passage about Jesus' brothers, you might say at the outset, "Most Roman Catholics believe that this passage refers to Jesus' cousins, while most Protestants believe that these were actual brothers. It really doesn't matter in our discussion. What matters is that people who were closest to Jesus did not believe him at this time in his ministry." If your group realizes that you will not be discussing differences of this nature, they will most likely not raise such issues.

How do we avoid going off on tangents? The best way to avoid tangents is to be well prepared. If you know what you hope to accomplish during the lesson time, you will be less likely to veer off course. As interesting as the tangents may be, the group as a whole will be more satisfied if you complete the lesson they planned on completing. Occasionally a lesson may be long, and you may want to do two lessons over the course of three meetings. Occasionally a member will have a crisis prayer request that is time-consuming. This should not be the norm, but the exception. In that case you may have to summarize some material or carry over a question or two to the next week.

Most lessons are designed to be studied in about an hour. If you have difficulty staying on schedule, you may want to write in the margin of your book what time you should begin each question. That will help you figure out why you are not able to finish, and will help you get back on track. It seems to be the nature of Bible study that the first questions in a lesson are given more time than the last questions. Try to cover all questions equally while acknowledging this reality.

What do I do if I run out of time? Stop. Break off mid-sentence, and say something like, "Oh, no, it's time to go." Better to leave your group wanting more than to bore them or continue past quitting time. Remember our goal is to whet people's appetite for studying the Bible, not to exhaust every possibility of what the Bible says. If you have nursery or other children's programs it is essential that you respect those leaders by stopping your discussion at the agreed-upon time. Even if you have a crisis in the group, go no more than ten minutes late, and even then, only with the permission of the group. This should be the exception, not the rule.

Will I ever stop feeling nervous? It is natural to feel nervous some of the time, especially near the beginning of the year. This is a ministry that centers on important issues of life and eternity. You would be wise to treat it with respect. Make sure that you pray for your group and for your leadership in it. Then make sure that you are well prepared. If you don't know or understand your material well, you are more likely to be nervous. But you should not feel excessively nervous all the time, year after year. If so, perhaps you would serve better in another ministry that is more suited to your spiritual giftedness.

How do we handle people who talk too little or too much? There will always be people who are more and less talkative in a group setting. Your goal is for roughly equal participation. Listening is a form of participation.

Don't assume that a quiet person is not learning. Using opening share questions is one way to encourage each member to talk. Very often they need to speak just once in the group situation before they begin to answer questions. Take time before or after the group meets to talk individually with quieter people. Usually it's best not to call on a quiet person in a group; if they want to talk, they will offer an answer. If you do call on people, make sure that you mention their name first, so that they will listen to the question more closely.

Handling the talkers is much more difficult. Try to sit next to them, and avoid eye contact and other encouraging body language. Occasionally you may need to ask if anyone else has something to add, or make a more general statement asking for other contributions to the discussions, such as, "What do the rest of you think? Has that been true in your life? Does anyone else have an opinion on that?" Don't tell them that they talk too much; they know. Pray for them. Some people are compulsive talkers and may need a one-on-one Bible study rather than a group study.

How do we deal with trite, superficial, or flippant responses? Sensitively challenge people to express their feelings and to relate their answers to real life through questions such as "How does this work out in real life? Is this easy to do day-by-day? How might we personalize this?" Ask people to paraphrase, or put an answer in their own words. Occasionally ask them to give an illustration of what they mean. If they are giving irrelevant information, gently ask how it fits in, or where they find it in the text. Sometimes people who have participated in other kinds of Bible studies are not accustomed to examining the text as closely as we do in Coffee Break Bible study.

How do we handle wrong answers? Probably one of the most difficult situations for a leader to manage well is when wrong answers are given. If you set the tone that several people answer each question you may be able to avoid addressing a wrong answer directly. What often happens in a group setting is that several possible answers are put forth, and the leader follows up on those that are correct or nearly right. The group then discusses the better answers and comes up with a correct answer.

If an answer seems quite far off-track, you may want to ask about it. Sensitively ask where they found that answer. Or say that you don't quite understand that answer, but wonder why they thought of it. They often will have a very good reason, which will clarify their thinking in your mind. Don't use this approach too often or you will stifle conversation. The discussion should be a discussion, not a question-and-answer session. In a free-flowing discussion, the flow of communication is among all group members, including the leader.

How do we handle those who object to what the Bible is saying? This is difficult. As much as we want people to believe what the Bible says, our job is to make clear what the Bible teaches, not to change hearts. That's the Holy Spirit's job. We want to encourage participation, including the expression of difficulty and doubts. Don't fall into the trap of becoming argumentative. Be calm and loving. You may occasionally be asked what you believe about a difficult issue. Gently explain what you think, and why, without being dogmatic. Don't give the impression that it is always easy to determine what the Bible is saying. We often must wrestle with the text.

How do we handle someone who is beginning to ask questions about a relationship with Christ? Rejoice. Give a general answer to the whole group, laying out the steps of salvation. Then offer to talk one-on-one with the individual outside the group setting. Someone who is being convicted by the Holy Spirit may appear agitated and restless; recognizing this sign may help you work with that person.

seven

THAT'S NOT ALL, FOLKS:
STORY HOUR AND LITTLE LAMBS

While Coffee Break, Story Hour, and Little Lambs are programs that can exist separately, most of the morning Coffee Break programs provide Story Hour for four- to six-year-olds and many provide Little Lambs for two- to three-year-olds. (Most evening Coffee Break groups do not provide children's programs.) The programs complement each other beautifully. Some mothers who would otherwise not attend a Bible study at a church may gladly bring their preschool children to Story Hour and Little Lambs and then be drawn into Coffee Break themselves. Others may come to share an hour of fellowship and study with other adults, but are able to do so only if they have a place to leave their small children. Don't underestimate the impact of the child on the family. As Story Hour children have shared their stories and activities at home, whole families have been drawn closer to the Lord.

Children's programs have their own unique value. It is wrong to think that the children's programs exist in order for the Coffee Break leaders to get the "real ministry" done. Evangelism with children is just as important as evangelism with adults. In fact, ministry with children is statistically a better investment of time and resources than ministry with adults. Each ministry is a valid one in its own right, but the ministries can have a large impact when used side-by-side.

The interactions between Coffee Break, Story Hour, and Little Lambs can be strengthened if each person values the ministry of the other. If all leaders believe that each ministry is equally important, you will have better success in communicating your needs to each other. Scheduling is probably the most difficult issue to work out. There must be give-and-take between the programs in order to develop a schedule, both yearly and weekly, that works well for everyone. Discussion will help. If any ministry dictates to the others, the balance is upset, and difficulties will surface.

Story Hour

Story Hour is an evangelistic program for preschool and kindergarten children ages four to six years old. The goal is to make God known simply and clearly, using the stories and teachings of the Bible in a way that children can understand. The desire is for each child to come to know God, to experience Jesus' love, and to respond to that love as the Holy Spirit works in each child's heart.

The Story Hour materials cover two years with forty lessons from both the Old and New Testaments in each year. The stories of Jesus' birth, death, and resurrection are told in both years. Generally the other stories are used on alternate years. The stories are divided by theme, the first lessons of each year being the Get Acquainted lessons, which introduce children to the Story Hour program, to the Bible, and to prayer. Special holiday lessons are included to help children celebrate selected secular holidays from a Christian perspective.

Session materials for each year are assembled into a program guide binder. The Story Hour program guide provides flexible session plans and includes a variety of learning activities. Songs, action rhymes, and patterns suggested in the learning activities are included in the binder. Music cassettes by Mary Rice Hopkins and Jon and Jacque Negus are also provided in the binder. (CDs are available for purchase.) Take-home story cards present the Bible stories in simple words that young children can understand. These cards are an excellent way to give the children their very own story Bible. All Story Hour leadership material is available from CRC Publications (1-800-333-8300).

Some Story Hour programs may have a Story Hour director; smaller programs may not. If no director is present, the responsibilities will be divided among the leaders. Your regional representative should be informed of the name of your Story Hour contact person.

Provide at least one leader for every five to seven children. Leaders should remain with the same group of children throughout the year to ensure a safe and predictable environment and to help leaders and children build relationships. It is very important that Story Hour leaders know who may pick up each child at the end of the session.

Grouping of children is the primary factor in determining space needs. There should be space for a large group of children for at least part of each session and separate space for smaller groups for the remainder of the time. Ideally, small groups should be no larger than about ten to fourteen children. You may wish to divide into smaller groups by age.

Regional representatives are available to schedule and conduct training workshops for Story Hour and Little Lambs. The three-hour workshop allows you to experience Story Hour and Little Lambs classes from a child's perspective. Call 1-800-333-8300 for the name of the regional representative nearest you.

Little Lambs

Little Lambs is a play curriculum designed to introduce two- and three-year-olds to God, his love, his Son, and his stories. Other goals of the program are to exemplify Jesus' love, to reduce separation anxiety, to lessen boredom or aggression in a nursery experience by providing an age-appropriate setting, and to lay down a solid foundation on which a relationship with the Lord can grow.

Every Little Lambs activity, song, and story was carefully chosen and written to fit the developmental level of the young child, recognizing that twos and threes learn by using all their senses. The children will learn many new things through play experiences. That is how young children learn best.

The Little Lambs curriculum parallels the Story Hour curriculum as much as possible. The first five lessons of each year lay the groundwork for the rest of the curriculum and give the children time to adjust to the leaders and to each other. The Little Lambs curriculum is available from CRC Publications (1-800-333-8300).

Twos and threes need and thrive on routines, so their schedule should remain consistent from week to week. Much of their time will be spent in play, but it is play with a purpose: to learn God's stories. Their playing is done at play centers, where leader and child play together as they talk about God's story for that day. Some of these centers are the playdough center, the art experience center, the game center, the house area, the little village, and the storybook center.

After picking up the toys, the children gather for a circle time in which they sing songs and do age-appropriate finger plays. The children then share a snack together and have story time. These stories are told on a story quilt and are usually repeated as often as the children want to hear them.

The leader who truly understands and loves the young child is key to the success of any Little Lambs program. The leader exemplifies God's love for the children and helps them feel good about coming to Little Lambs.

Two resources that will further acquaint you with Story Hour and Little Lambs are the booklet *Little Ones Need Jesus* (a part of the Coffee Break Core Values series) and a free informational brochure, *What's Growing?*. Both are available from CRC Publications (1-800-333-8300).

eight

NEED DIRECTION?
THE DIRECTOR'S ROLE

Because Coffee Break groups have been meeting since the early 1970s, some programs are large and well-established. Many of your current policies and procedures may have been determined by previous leaders and directors. On the other hand, your church may be launching this ministry for the first time, and one leader has been designated as the director. In many churches the duties of director are shared among two or more leaders. One of those leaders should be the contact person for the regional representative. When leadership changes, be sure to inform your regional representative of those changes or call the Coffee Break office at 1-888-644-0814.

The following duties should be the responsibility of the director.

1. Pray that the Holy Spirit will touch the lives of all who participate in the Coffee Break ministry, including those in Story Hour, Little Lambs, nursery, kitchen, and other support staff. Lay a foundation of prayer for all the leaders.

2. Guard the purpose of Coffee Break. Remember that Coffee Break is a small-group, inductive Bible study program for the purpose of leading people to a personal relationship with Jesus Christ. Make sure that every leader in your program understands and firmly holds to this purpose.

3. Maintain effective communication with the church's leaders, if this is a church-based program. If you are holding a Coffee Break group in your home, on your own, you would be wise to inform your church's leaders also. Tell your church's leaders that you will communicate regularly and that you value their input and support. Learn the type of reporting they prefer, how frequently those reports should be made, and the standards or requirements for selecting new leaders. Do you need approval from the church's governing body? Are leaders required to be members of your church? Submit the names of your leaders to your church council for official approval, if necessary.

4. Keep your pastor informed about your ministry. Let the pastor know that you value prayer, input, and support. Encourage your pastor to be available to Coffee Break members who may need professional help that you are not able to give. Ask your pastor to be visible when you meet, in a low-key, nonthreatening way, so that group members will not be intimidated. Developing a casual relationship with group members may help dispel their stereotypes of clergy.

5. Encourage your leaders to attend training workshops and the biennial Coffee Break convention so that they are well prepared for and encouraged in their ministry.

6. Arrange for ongoing leaders' meetings throughout the ministry season. Help the leaders renew their sense of purpose and oneness of ministry, recharging their spirits for ministry. Include time for relaxation, Bible study, and sharing and praying together. Enjoy good food. Discuss your goals, your requirements for leadership, and details regarding your Bible studies. Encourage each other as you minister together, and be sure to include times of celebration. You may be able to arrange an overnight leaders' retreat to kick off your ministry year. Drawing away from the hectic pace of daily living to focus on refreshment from Christ and one another is an effective means for bonding the staff together.

7. Be available to fill in for leaders when needed or arrange for a substitute.

The director does not have to perform all of the following duties, but should make sure that each of them is performed.

1. Order study guides and leader guides. Each leader will need a leader's guide and a study guide. Each participant will need a study guide. Order additional material when necessary. All resources for Coffee Break, Story Hour, and Little Lambs are available from CRC Publications (1-800-333-8300).

2. Make the necessary arrangements if you are using childcare. Help the person in charge to develop guidelines that may be shared with group members, such as labeling bottles and bags with the name of their child, not bringing children who have contagious illnesses to the nursery, making sure that nursery staff know where to locate parents if their child needs them, and so on. If you serve the children snacks, make sure their caretakers know.

3. Arrange for kitchen helpers, if necessary, or make a treat sign-up sheet. Figure out how to handle cleanup.

4. Check to make sure the rooms are set up properly.

5. Decide how to handle registration, and make sure that someone is in charge of filling out registration cards for those who join mid-year.

6. Make sure that you have name tags. Even when your group members all know each other it is helpful to wear them every time. Then when newcomers arrive you won't have to scramble to get them.

7. Arrange to have signs posted and greeters available for the first few meetings.

8. Decide how those who are attending will be divided into groups. In established programs this is a big task. This always should be done with a deep sense of responsibility and much prayer. Seek a balance as you consider the various ages, the levels of spiritual maturity, the talkers and the shy, the sparklers, the difficult, and so on. Try to foresee and avoid possible personality conflicts. Realize at the outset that you will make mistakes.

    In most cases, the group gels during the year to the point where members are reluctant to break their circle, but do shuffle the groups at the beginning of the next season. Usually the same bonding takes place and everyone benefits from the change. If possible, reassign people in pairs so there is at least one familiar face in the new group.

9. Make announcements, recognize birthdays, and so on at the beginning or end of the session. Some large groups have a wrap-up session together at the end of the small group time.

10. Arrange for social events, such as a Christmas party. This may be done by committee, and is often something in which group members can participate.

11. Plan the schedule for the season. Determine "snow day" policies if necessary. Check the local school calendars so you can work around them.

12. Decide if you will have prayer partners between leaders or from the congregation or elsewhere.

13. Determine and oversee your budget.

14. Plan your promotions.

15. Maintain records of personnel, membership, advertising methods, Bible studies used, and dates and kinds of special events.

16. If your leaders work on fund-raisers for expenses, make plans.

17. Decide what you will do during your first session together.

18. Decide how you will spend your time in the group setting.

nine

LOOKING BACK:
WHY COFFEE BREAK WORKS

In 1970, Coffee Break started as one Bible study group in a single church. Other churches expressed interest, and programs were added one by one. Leaders soon reported that many participants had made commitments to Christ or reaffirmed their faith, and many others had experienced revitalized spiritual growth and become more active in their own churches. Many participants began visiting the worship services with their families and inquiring about church membership.

Today, more than thirty years later, over a thousand churches representing more than forty denominations all over Canada and the United States have developed Coffee Break Bible studies. Groups are starting in several other countries, and materials are being published in both the Korean and Spanish languages. New groups start every year, and churches report that their memberships are increasing as a result. Clearly the Coffee Break ministry is effective and fruitful.

What makes Coffee Break so effective? To answer this question, we must look at the heart of the Coffee Break program itself, identifying the principles on which it operates.

The Power of Prayer

Coffee Break works because those who begin and continue leading the ministry are people of prayer. As the leaders pray about the ministry they are sensitized to God's leading and begin to follow it. As they carry out God's will for the program they feel a sense of peace in knowing that they are doing what God wants them to do. A booklet that should be on the reading list of any Coffee Break leader is *The Priority of Prayer* by Edith Bajema. To order, call CRC Publications (1-800-333-8300).

The Power of God's Word

Coffee Break is based on the premise that there is immense power when the written Word is applied to people's hearts by the working of the Holy Spirit. Regular exposure to the truth of God's Word will change people's lives, perhaps slowly and almost unnoticeably at first, but the changes will occur. There is no more effective tool for evangelism than exposure to God's Word. Coffee Break Bible study is valuable for precisely this reason: it brings people into sustained contact with the transforming power of the Word. We have faith in the power of God's Word to renew people's hearts, to bring them hope and new life.

Through the pages of that Word, Coffee Break participants become acquainted with the lives and words of women and men who testify to the reality and power of God's grace. These words proclaim God's love and his offer of salvation in his Son, Jesus Christ. Their voices, recorded in the Bible, are insistent and persuasive because the Holy Spirit inspired them and applies them to the hearts of those who listen.

God's Word changes lives by exposing sin. The writer of Hebrews describes the convicting power of the Word: "The Word of God is living and active. Sharper than any double-edged sword, it penetrates even to dividing soul and spirit, joints and marrow; it judges the thoughts and attitudes of the heart" (4:12). God's Word penetrates to the center of a person's being and exposes the hidden depths of the secret self. In this way God strips away elaborate masks and cover-ups, laying bare the sinful nature. This helps unbelievers to take the first step toward salvation: acknowledging their sin and guilt before God. This awareness of sin does not usually come through a brief conversation or a one-time evangelistic encounter, but through continued and consistent exposure to God's Word such as the Coffee Break group provides.

God's Word also changes lives through the good news of the gospel, which offers salvation by grace through faith in Christ. This is good news because it answers the problem of our sin. Paul says that the gospel is "the power of God for the salvation of everyone who believes" (Rom. 1:16). When people hear this good news, the power of God works in human hearts and draws them to salvation. This explains the effectiveness of Coffee Break Bible study groups, which allow participants to hear the good news and open their hearts to God's power working in them.

God's Word also matures the faith of the new believer. Studying the Bible helps equip new believers for their walk in the Christian life. It is one of God's tools for spiritual growth. As Paul says, "All Scripture is inspired by God and is useful for teaching, for reproof, for correction, and for training in righteousness, so that everyone who belongs to God may be proficient, equipped for every good work" (2 Tim. 3:16-17, NRSV). The Coffee Break group is a place where training and equipping can happen, maturing new believers into active participants in the church through the power of God's Word.

In sum, Coffee Break works because God's Word is effective in pointing out sin, in revealing the Savior, and in directing spiritual growth.

The Power of Love

The Coffee Break group relies not only on the power of prayer and the written Word but also on another power that draws unbelievers to God. That power is love. Just look at Paul's words: "God demonstrates his own love for us in this: While we were still sinners, Christ died for us" (Rom. 5:8). God reached out to us in love when we were far from him. Love is a mighty force.

As a response to God's love, the Coffee Break leader will exemplify Christ's love to the world. (Every leader should read the Core Values series booklet *Leading with Love* by Barbara Brouwer. To order, call CRC Publications, 1-800-333-8300.) Relationships with group members are opportunities to show God's love to others. The love shown in Coffee Break groups is magnetic, dynamic, and personal. As group members experience that accepting and caring love from each other, they are drawn to respond to the gospel.

The power of love, expressed in concrete and specific ways in the small group, draws people irresistibly to the heart of God, from which all love comes. Group members feel a sense of belonging because they are known as individuals. They are given an opportunity to learn by giving and receiving honest feedback. They are supported in times of crisis and pain. They are enabled to resist sinful or addictive behaviors to a greater degree than they would alone. They are more willing to take steps toward making changes in their lives than those who are not part of a group. They are better able to make decisions and solve problems in the context of the small group. The Holy Spirit brings refreshment and healing to others because the Spirit brings God's love.

The Power of the Mobilized Church

Another reason that the Coffee Break ministry works is that it utilizes the power of the church. Most Coffee Break groups meet in a church building for convenience. The meeting rooms are usually comfortable, there is often plenty of parking, kitchen facilities are usually available, and there is often room for Story Hour, Little Lambs, and nursery. If the Coffee Break ministry is part of a church's strategy to reach the lost, many people in the congregation will want to pray for the program. (Provide the congregation with copies of the Core Values series booklet *Linking to the Lost*. Call 1-800-333-8300 to order.)

Because the Coffee Break climate is low-key and less threatening than a formal worship service, the Bible study can draw into the church building those people who would normally stay away. The contact with the church also makes it more likely that those who become new believers through the Bible study will consider membership in that church. (See the Core Values series booklet *Linking to the Church*. Call 1-800-333-8300 to order.) In addition, many people feel drawn to be part of an organization with a wide array of programs and activities; therefore being connected to a church through Coffee Break may appeal to them. Sometime along the way they may also attend a worship service.

Coffee Break is led by church members rather than clergy. Many people outside the church would hesitate to come to a Bible study led by a pastor, but will attend a group led by a church member. Church members may also be more willing to invite their non-Christian friends to a group led by someone who may be perceived as less intimidating than the pastor. Involving church members in ministry is a sound biblical principle. "Like good stewards of the manifold grace of God, serve one another with whatever gift each of you has received" (1 Pet. 4:10, NRSV). Members of Christ's church are called to be actively involved in Christ's work, the ministry of reconciling the world to God. Coffee Break Bible study offers the opportunity for people to develop their spiritual gifts and use them in outreach.

People are spiritually hungry; they have interest in knowing God and in finding out what the Bible says. Most people also yearn for close relationships. Coffee Break small groups offer both these things. A low-key Bible study whose purpose is simply to discover what the Bible says allows people to see that others struggle with the same questions they have. As group members grow more comfortable in the loving, open environment of the small group, they will begin to hear the gospel's call to salvation in Jesus. With God's leading, such Bible study groups may be the best way to reach this segment of society with God's answers to life's problems.